Coral
REEFS

By Sydnie Meltzer Kleinhenz

CELEBRATION PRESS
Pearson Learning Group

The following people from **Pearson Learning Group**
have contributed to the development of this product:

Joan Mazzeo, Lisa Arcuri **Design** | **Editorial** Betsy Niles, Linette Mathewson
Christine Fleming **Marketing** | **Publishing Operations** Jennifer Van Der Heide
Production Laura Benford-Sullivan
Content Area Consultants Dr. Amy Rabb-Liu and Dr. Charles Liu

The following people from **DK** have
contributed to the development of this product:

Art Director Rachael Foster

Clive Savage, Carole Oliver **Design** | **Managing Editor** Scarlett O'Hara
Helen McFarland **Picture Research** | **Editorial** Amanda Rayner, Kate Pearce
Richard Czapnik, Andy Smith **Cover Design** | **Production** Rosalind Holmes
Trevor Day **Consultant** | **DTP** David McDonald

Dorling Kindersley would like to thank: Peter Visscher for original artwork, Ed Merritt for the map, Johnny Pau for additional cover design work.

Picture Credits: Corbis: Lawson Wood 24tr. FLPA - Images of nature: D Fleetham/Silvestris 10cl; Earthviews 17tl; Gerard Lacz 13cl; Silvestris 16cr. Getty Images:; Stephen Frink 30b; Art Wolfe 27b. Malcolm Hey: 11tr, 14-15. N.H.P.A.: A.N.T 8-9; Bill Wood 12tr; Norbert Wu 16bl. Nature Picture Library: Jurgen Freud 10bl, 26tr. NOAA: Florida Keys National Marine Sanctuary 10tl; Dr. James P. McVey/ NOAA Sea Grant Program 4tr, 24bl, 25tl; NOAA Restoration Centre/Erik Zobrist 29tr. Oxford Scientific Films: David Fleetham 1, 11cr; Mark Webster 4-5; Norbert Wu 25c. Rex Features: Brett Inman 28b. Science Photo Library: 12bl; Georgette Douwma 21b, 29b; Andrew J Martinez 10br; Peter Scoones 7c; Nancy Sefton 11bl. Woodfall Wild Images: Sue Scott 22tr, 22-23; Lawson Wood 5bc. Cover: ImageState/Pictor: Georgette Douwma back l. N.H.P.A.: A.N.T front t. Science Photo Library: Peter Scoones front bl.

All other images: Dorling Kindersley © 2005. For further information see www.dkimages.com

ISBN: 0-7652-5223-6

Color reproduction by Colourscan, Singapore
Printed and bound in China by Leo Paper Products Ltd.
1 2 3 4 5 6 7 8 9 10   08 07 06 05 04

1-800-321-3106
www.pearsonlearning.com

Contents

Coral Reefs and Polyps

Coral reefs are like underwater cities. They are full of energy and activity. More species of sea creatures and plants live on coral reefs than anywhere else in the ocean.

A coral reef may look like a rock formation on the sea floor. It's not. It's really made up of millions of tiny **coral polyps**. Polyps live together in huge groups. These groups make up a coral reef.

These polyps are part of a coral reef.

What Are Coral Polyps?

Until about 200 years ago, scientists were not sure what polyps were. Some thought that coral polyps were plants. They are actually small, soft-bodied animals. Some coral polyps grow a hard outer structure called an **exoskeleton**. Most polyps are only about one-quarter inch across. It takes millions of these tiny animals to form a coral reef.

Coral reefs are home to a huge variety of colorful sea creatures. Reefs are often called "rain forests of the sea."

Hard Coral Polyp

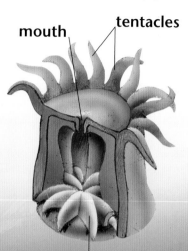

mouth

tentacles

exoskeleton

From Polyp to Coral Reef

Coral polyps make up the top layer of a coral reef. The lower part of the reef is made up of polyp exoskeletons.

There are about 230,000 square miles of coral reef in the world today. It takes a long time for a coral reef to form. Studies have shown that, on average, a coral clump grows outward about an inch or so a year. At this rate, it would take more than ten years for a new clump to produce material about the size of a soccer ball.

Cross Section of a Branching Coral

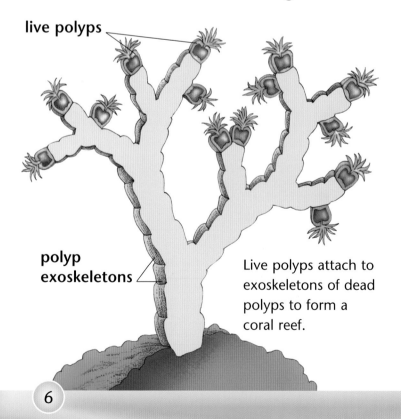

live polyps

polyp exoskeletons

Live polyps attach to exoskeletons of dead polyps to form a coral reef.

How a Coral Reef Grows

young polyps

sea floor

1. Young polyps attach to the sea floor.

polyp

exoskeleton

2. As the polyp grows it forms an exoskeleton.

3. When the polyp dies it leaves behind its exoskeleton.

living polyp

new exoskeleton

old exoskeleton

4. New polyps grow on top and lay down a new exoskeleton. The coral reef builds.

Living Polyps

Coral reefs develop in clear, warm, shallow waters. These ocean **habitats** are rich in a variety of life forms. For a coral reef to grow, polyps need food. However, polyps can't freely move about to get food. Instead, they use their **tentacles** to catch food as it floats by.

Polyps eat **plankton**, which is made up of many different kinds of tiny sea plants and creatures that float in the shallow ocean. A polyp first stings the plankton with its tentacles. It then pushes the plankton into its mouth.

Some polyps also get food from **algae** (AL-jee), a kind of plantlike plankton. Some forms of algae actually live inside the bodies of coral polyps.

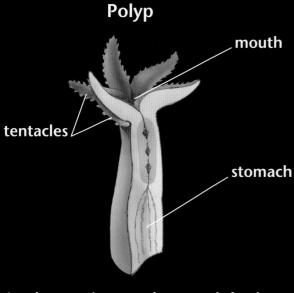

Polyp

mouth

tentacles

stomach

A polyp uses its tentacles to push food into its mouth and down to its stomach.

Living Together

Coral polyps and algae work as a team. The algae make food for the polyps. In return, the polyps give the algae a place to live. This type of teamwork is called **symbiosis**.

pillar coral

cup coral

brain coral

Types of Coral

All types of coral polyps grow in a similar way. However, different polyps form corals of many shapes and sizes. There are more than 2,500 different kinds of coral.

Corals can be hard or soft. Hard coral polyps have exoskeletons. The exoskeletons help make up a reef. There are about 600 kinds of hard coral.

This spectacular reef includes many different types of coral.

Soft coral polyps do not have exoskeletons. So, they are not reef builders. However, these corals are still an important part of a reef habitat.

Some corals look like tree branches, tiny pipes, or mushrooms. Other corals look like fans, feathers, or lace. One kind of hard coral looks like a human brain. Coral can also be many colors. It can be pink, yellow, orange, or rich purple, with colors so bright that they seem to glow.

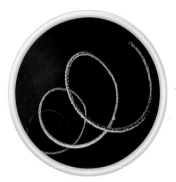

spiral coral

toadstool coral

fan coral

Coral Reef Creatures

Warm, sunlit waters and lots of hiding places attract many creatures to a coral reef. In a reef ecosystem, there is a great variety of creatures. In fact, there are more kinds of animals in coral reefs than in any habitat on Earth except rain forests.

With all that sea life, there's much activity. Some fish feed on the coral polyps or graze on algae and plankton. Bigger fish feed on smaller fish. Every creature looks for a meal. Luckily, a variety of sea life means there is something for everyone.

Cleanup Crew
Certain small fish nibble **parasites**, and food bits off big fish. This is all part of the reef food chain. Here, a small wrasse feeds in the mouth of a grouper.

Coral Reef Food Chain

Plankton

Tiny Animals

plant
plankton

coral
polyp

The Coral Reef Food Chain

   Coral reef creatures are part of a **food chain**. A food chain is the way that living things gain nourishment. On a reef, a food chain starts with algae and plankton. Algae make food using the energy from sunlight. The energy in food is passed along the food chain.

   Some fish eat plankton, including algae, for energy and nourishment. Then, larger fish and animals eat these fish. These larger fish and animals are called **predators** because they hunt and kill other animals for food. The predators gain their energy from the fish they eat.

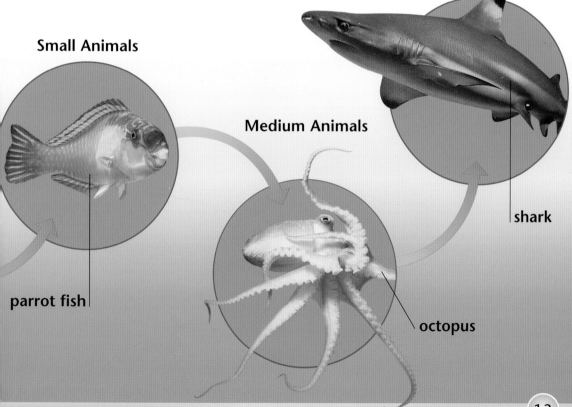

Large Animals

Small Animals

Medium Animals

shark

parrot fish

octopus

Mandarin fish are some of the most colorful fish on the reef.

Fish of the Coral Reef

Nearly one-third of the world's species of fish live in coral reefs. Most coral reef fish are brilliantly colored. In the crowded reef, these colors help the fish to recognize their own kind. Colors, shapes, markings, and other features help fish to find food, hide, and defend themselves.

The mandarin fish is covered with bright orange, yellow, blue, and green stripes and dots. The mandarin's colors warn large fish to stay away from it. It is also covered with a bad-tasting slime.

Butterfly fish poke their long snouts into coral and pull off the soft polyps for food.

The angelfish's narrow body helps it dart easily through the coral.

A butterfly fish has clever markings as well as vivid colors. A black spot near its tail looks like an eye. It confuses predators and helps the fish escape.

The bright colors of an angelfish attract a mate. Mated pairs stay together and, like guard dogs, chase other angelfish from their territory.

The lionfish has spines that stick out like a lion's mane. The spines hold a powerful poison. Predators stay away so they won't get poisoned.

The lionfish's bright colors act as a warning. Watch out for poisonous spines!

Hiding for Safety

A sea horse wraps its tail around coral and stays in the same place for long periods of time. It can't swim quickly away from predators. Instead it protects itself with **camouflage**. It changes color to match the coral where it rests.

Predators of the Coral Reef

Sharks, barracudas, manta rays, and moray eels are among the largest predators of the coral reef. Each has a different way of hunting prey. Moray eels hide in caves, and then rush out to snatch up lobsters, crabs, and fish.

Reef sharks eat similar creatures. They hunt at night, swimming over the surface of the reef to catch their prey. Like moray eels, sharks use smell, sight, and sense vibrations in the water to find their prey.

The manta ray was once known to sailors as a "devil fish" because of the "horns" on its head. These "horns" are actually fins that guide plankton and shrimp into its wide mouth.

Barracudas often hunt in groups, or schools. They use their razor-sharp teeth to bite at whatever moves quickly. Barracudas eat mostly fish, including poisonous ones.

barracuda

reef shark

moray eel

manta ray

Massive Manta

This picture shows the size of a manta ray as compared to humans. It can stretch more than 20 feet wide and can weigh more than 2 tons.

Sea Anemones and Sea Urchins

Both sea anemones and sea urchins can protect themselves from predators. Sea anemones may look like beautiful flowers. In fact, they are really animals related to coral polyps and jellyfish. They catch their prey by using stinging cells in their tentacles. When a small fish touches the anemone's tentacles, it is paralyzed. Then the tentacles move the fish to the anemone's mouth.

Some anemones attach themselves to the reef. Some bury their bodies in sand. Others get plucked up by hermit crabs, who wear them to camouflage their shells.

Unlike other fish, clownfish are not harmed by the anemone's tentacles.

yellow anemone

bubble anemone

clownfish

fire anemone

The sea urchin looks like a pincushion. Its body is covered with spines that can move. The spines are attached to a shell-like surface, called a **test**. Sea urchins move on tube feet and scare predators away with their spines.

Sea urchins graze on seaweed. This helps keep the seaweed from growing out of control. They also eat other types of algae and small animals. The sea urchin has a sneaky predator—the triggerfish. A triggerfish can blow a stream of water at a sea urchin to knock it over. Then the triggerfish eats through the underside where there are no spines.

Sea Urchin

test

tube feet

spines

mouth

The tube feet of these sea urchins have suckers that grip onto the surface of a rock or reef.

Octopus and Cuttlefish

The octopus and the cuttlefish can change color to avoid predators or to lure their prey. The octopus is a master of disguise. To avoid morays and sharks, it puffs up to look bigger or changes color to camouflage itself. It also changes its colors according to mood. For example, it might turn white when frightened or blue when angry.

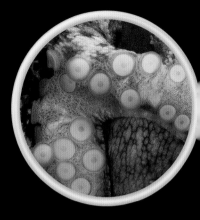

Suction cups are arranged in rows on the underside of an octopus's tentacles.

An octopus uses its eight arms to catch its prey—usually a fish or a crab. Some octopuses have more than 1,000 suction cups on the underside of their arms. These suction cups give the octopus a sense of touch and taste. Experiments have shown that an octopus is so clever that it can figure out how to unscrew a jar lid to reach food.

An octopus sometimes hides itself in underwater caves.

A cuttlefish glides through the water by using the wide rippling fin that surrounds its body. When it is frightened, it shoots a dark liquid, or ink, from its body. This helps it to escape its predators. People used to catch the cuttlefish and use its ink for writing.

Both the cuttlefish and the octopus hunt at night. Their eyes are positioned so they can see in almost every direction. The cuttlefish grabs a shrimp or a crab with its two tentacles. Its eight arms help guide the food to its mouth.

A cuttlefish can confuse predators by rapidly flashing different colors.

Crabs, Lobsters, and Shrimp

Crabs, lobsters, and shrimp also make coral reefs their home. These animals have hard, shell-like exoskeletons instead of bones. As an animal grows, its exoskeleton becomes too small and splits. The animal climbs out and eats the shell, which is nourishing. These animals stay well hidden from predators until a new exoskeleton develops and hardens. Cracks in a coral reef provide good hiding places from hungry sharks and octopuses.

As crabs get older, they shed their shells and grow new ones.

Squat lobsters use their large claws as weapons when they fight.

The reef provides protection as well as food for lobsters, crabs, and shrimp. These animals eat small living creatures, but they are also **scavengers**. They eat dead plants and animals. This tidies up the reef.

Lobsters sometimes eat other lobsters, too. They also fight with their claws to defend their territory. Crabs eat everything from algae to sea urchins. They break open the sea urchins with their hard claws.

The strawberry shrimp prefers to eat parasites from the bodies of large fish. When it wants a meal, it does a dance to show the fish that it's ready!

Clever Cleaner

The bright color of a strawberry shrimp attracts fish who need cleaning. Then the strawberry shrimp eats the parasites off the fish.

Living Shells

The empty shells you find on a beach were once the hard outer coverings around living, soft-bodied animals. Many shelled animals get their food from plankton and algae that live on or near the reef. These animals are protected by their hard outer shells. They also hide in crevices in the reef.

murex shell

Some shelled animals, like the murex, use camouflage to hide. Their shells can look like coral. Other animals, like the cowrie shell, can hide among clumps of coral.

A cowrie is a kind of sea snail that crawls along coral reefs.

Some shelled animals have other ways to protect themselves. The cone snail has a poisonous dart in its mouth. It uses this dart to catch prey and to protect itself.

The giant clam is far too big to hide inside the coral. It can measure more than 5 feet across and weigh more than 500 pounds. It watches for danger with its tiny eyes. It then quickly closes its hinged shell for protection.

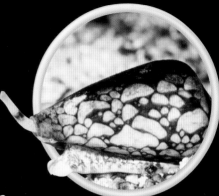

cone snail

The giant blue clam can grow almost as large as an adult human.

Coral Reefs Around the World

Coral reefs exist in several different parts of the world. Most of them are found in the warm seas that lie near the equator. Polyps need shallow water to grow, so coral reefs are often near land. There are three different type of coral reefs: **atoll reefs**, **fringing reefs**, and **barrier reefs**.

atoll reef   lagoon

The Maldive Islands in the Indian Ocean are atoll reefs.

World Reef Map

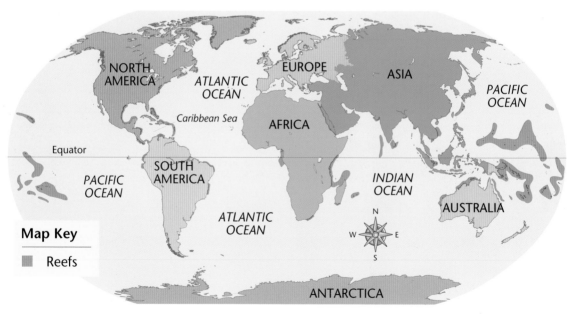

NORTH AMERICA

EUROPE

ASIA

ATLANTIC OCEAN

PACIFIC OCEAN

Caribbean Sea

AFRICA

Equator

PACIFIC OCEAN

SOUTH AMERICA

INDIAN OCEAN

ATLANTIC OCEAN

AUSTRALIA

N
W   E
S

Map Key

Reefs

ANTARCTICA

Most reefs are in the Pacific and Indian Oceans and the Caribbean Sea.

An atoll reef is a ring-shaped reef around a **lagoon**. Unlike other types of reefs, atolls may be far from land. An atoll develops over thousands of years around a volcanic island. Eventually, the volcanic island sinks below the ocean. Later, parts of the atoll may rise above water and become islands themselves.

A fringing reef is right next to the shoreline. A barrier reef also follows the shoreline, but it is separated from the land by a wide lagoon.

shoreline   fringing reef

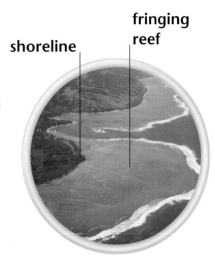

This reef in the Pacific Ocean is a fringing reef.

This island of Bora-Bora in the Pacific Ocean is surrounded by a barrier reef.

lagoon

barrier reef

The Great Barrier Reef

The Great Barrier Reef is the largest coral reef in the world. It stretches for 1,260 miles. It is made up of many separate reefs near the northeast coast of Australia. This habitat is home to thousands of species of fish, coral, and other animals.

The Great Barrier Reef

Life Around the Great Barrier Reef

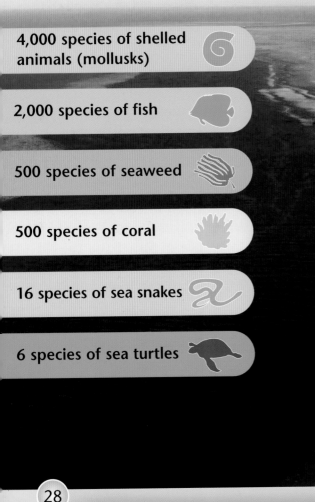

4,000 species of shelled animals (mollusks)

2,000 species of fish

500 species of seaweed

500 species of coral

16 species of sea snakes

6 species of sea turtles

The Great Barrier Reef runs alongside the northeast coast of Queensland, Australia.

Protecting Reefs

Coral reefs have been around for millions of years, but today many reefs are in danger. One threat to these reefs is human activity, especially overfishing. A second threat is the physical damage people do to reefs. Just touching a reef with a hand or foot can kill the coral polyps beneath.

Coral reefs are also threatened by the effects of pollution. Water pollution has harmed or killed many creatures. Global warming has caused some parts of the ocean to become too warm for some reefs to survive.

Caring for Coral
Humans must be careful around coral reefs. Fishing or collecting shells can damage a reef.

Pollution can cause coral to lose its color. This is called bleached coral.

Coral reefs are one of the most important habitats in the world. It's no wonder that people are now working hard to preserve and restore them. Fishermen are protecting the balance of predator and prey by keeping better track of what they catch. Tourists are being careful not to remove animals and shells from the reef.

With help, the reefs can slowly rebuild. These cities under the sea can grow and continue to be lively and healthy homes for thousands of plants and creatures.

Glossary

algae	plantlike creatures that grow in the water and use sunlight to make food
atoll reefs	ring-shaped reefs around a lagoon
barrier reefs	reefs along the shore that are separated from the land by a lagoon
camouflage	a disguise to blend with the surroundings
coral polyps	individual coral animals
coral reefs	platforms or ridges of coral at or near the ocean surface
exoskeleton	a hard outer covering supporting an animal's insides
food chain	the passing of food energy between members of a community of living things
fringing reefs	reefs that form along shorelines
habitats	places where animals and plants live together
lagoon	an area of shallow water separated from the sea
parasites	creatures that benefit by living in or on other creatures, which they harm
plankton	tiny plants and animals floating in the ocean
predators	animals that hunt and kill other animals for food
scavengers	animals that eat dead animals
symbiosis	a partnership that benefits two different kinds of living things
tentacles	long, flexible body parts, such as octopus arms
test	a hard external covering on certain animals, such as sea urchins

Index